AF481074

BIG VOWEL BOOK FOR LITTLE READERS

Reading for Kindergarten
Children's Reading & Writing Books

Speedy Publishing LLC

40 E. Main St. #1156

Newark, DE 19711

www.speedypublishing.com

Copyright 2017

A Vowel is a speech sound made with the vocal tract open.

The study of vowel sounds is important to students' early reading and writing skills.

Practice Printing the Vowels

A a

A is for airplane.

Ee

E is for eight.

I is for insect.

O is for ocean.

U u

U is for ukulele.

Color the
pictures and read
their names.

Aa

Ee

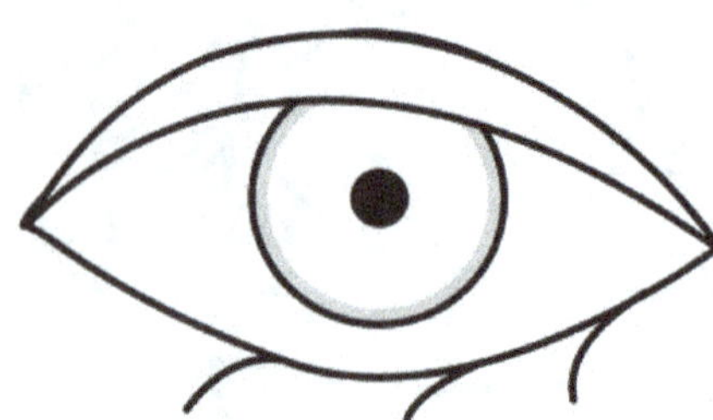

Eye

Eggplant

Easter Egg

Elephant

Ii
Ice
Ice cream
Ivy
Igloo

Oo

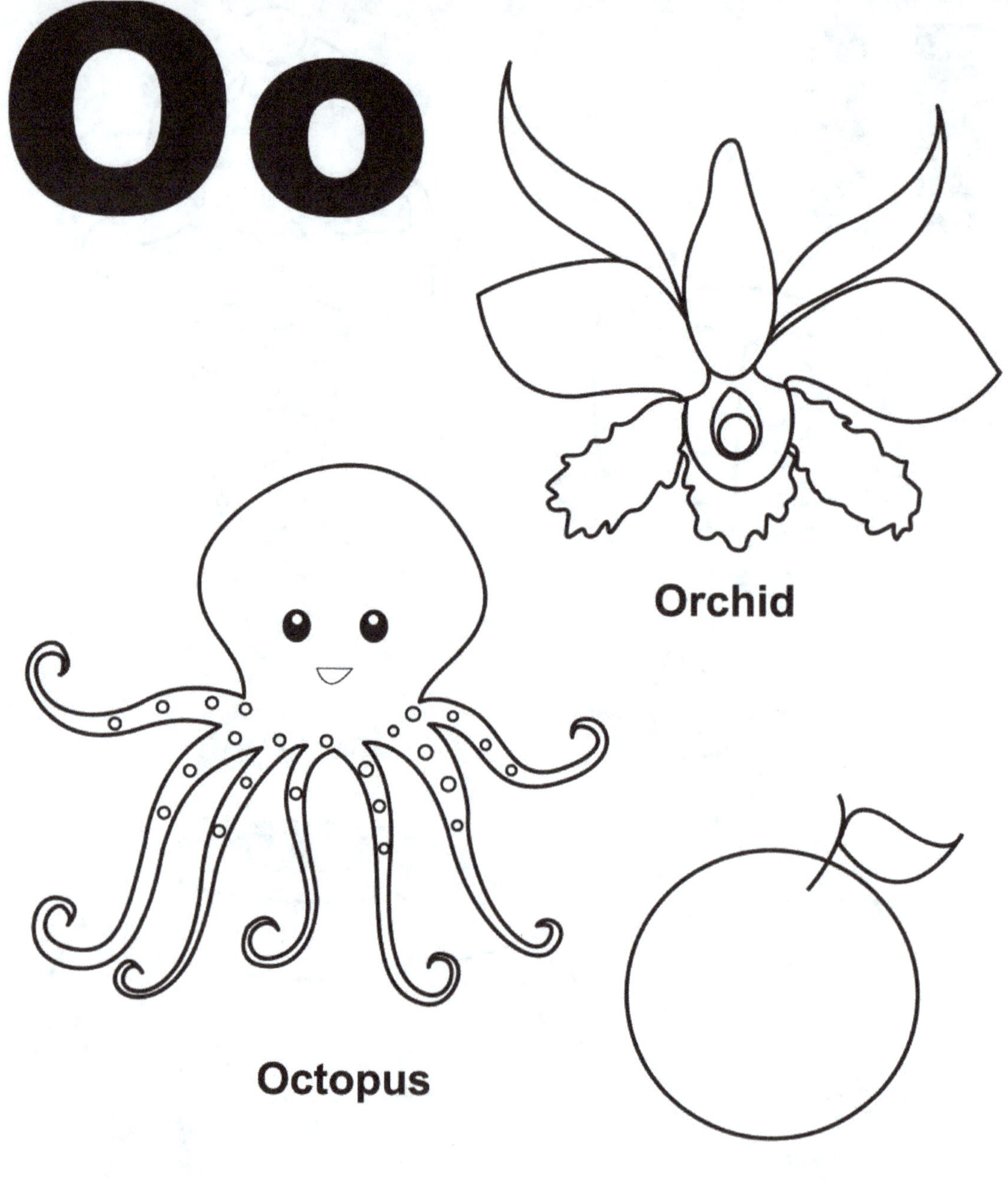

Octopus

Orchid

Orange

Uu

Utensils

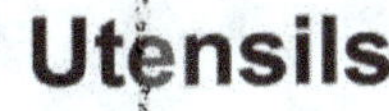

Umbrella

Unicorn

Practice tracing
the word.
Say the word.

A a

Apple

Apple

Apple

Apple

Apple

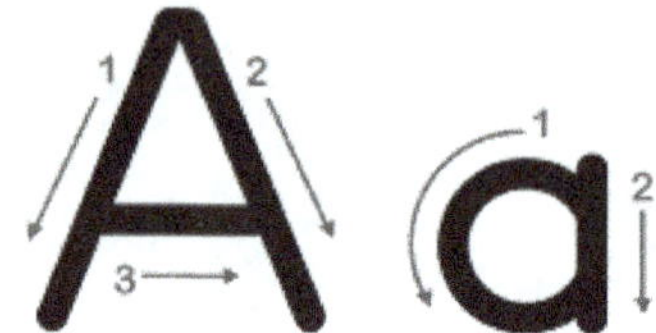

Ant

Ant

Ant

Ant

Ant

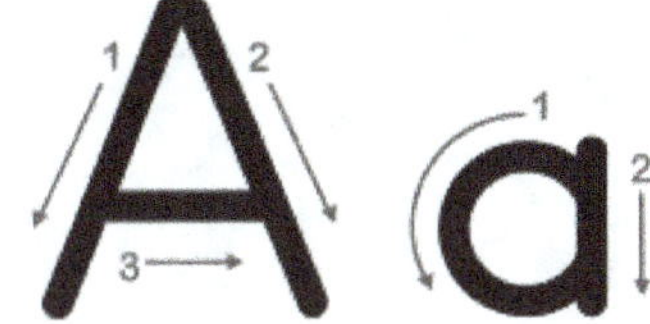

Angel

Angel

Angel

Angel

Angel

E e
Elephant
Elephant   Elephant
Elephant   Elephant

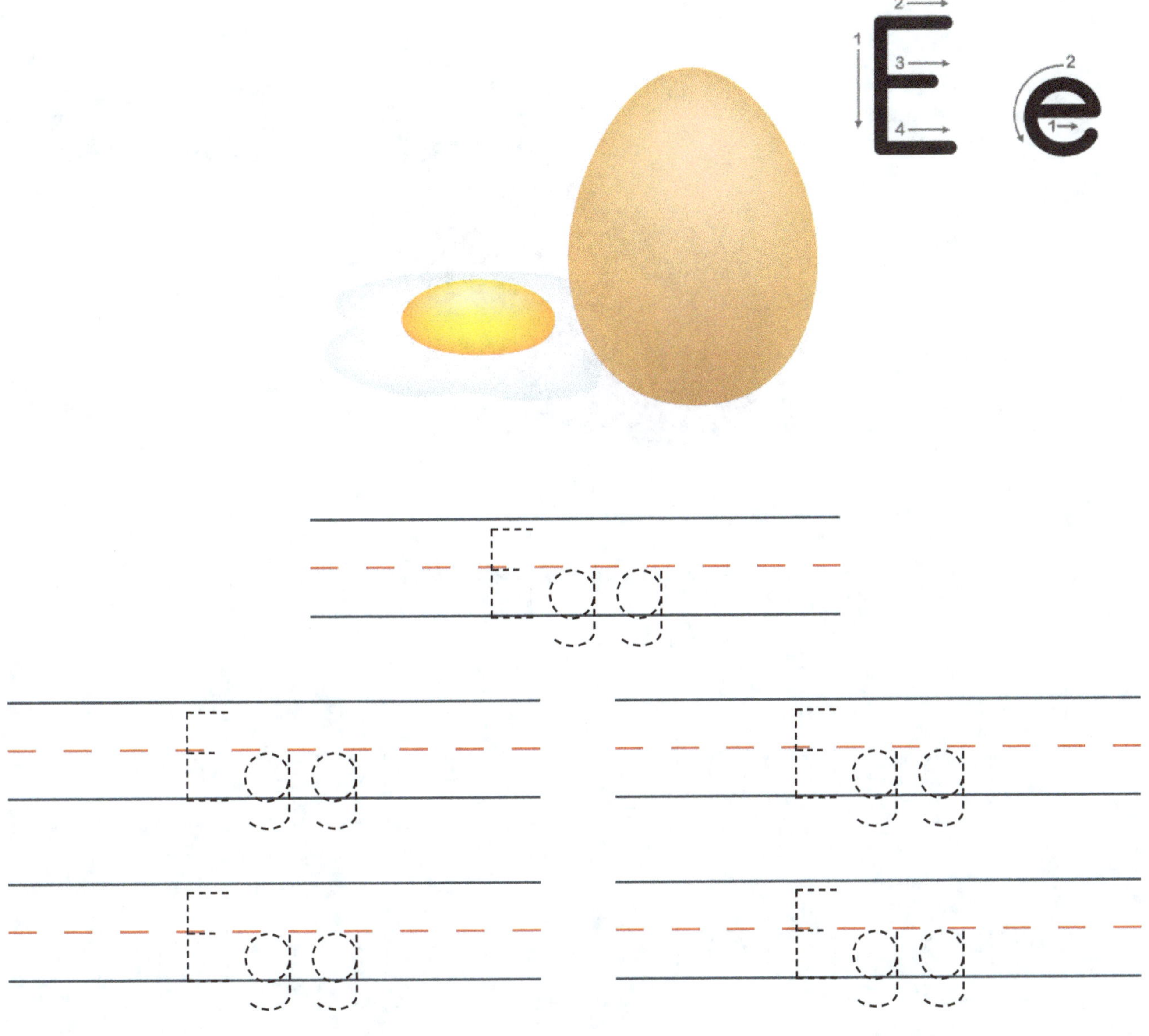

E
e
Egg
Egg
Egg
Egg
Egg

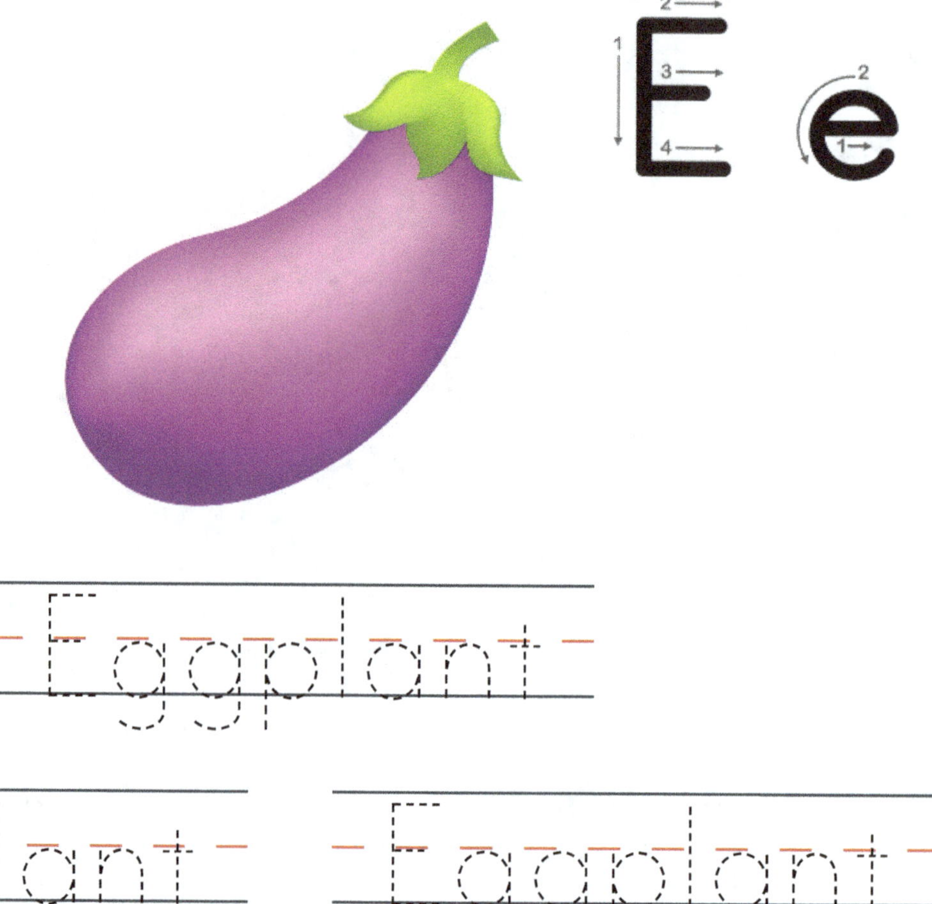

E e

Eggplant

Eggplant   Eggplant

Eggplant   Eggplant

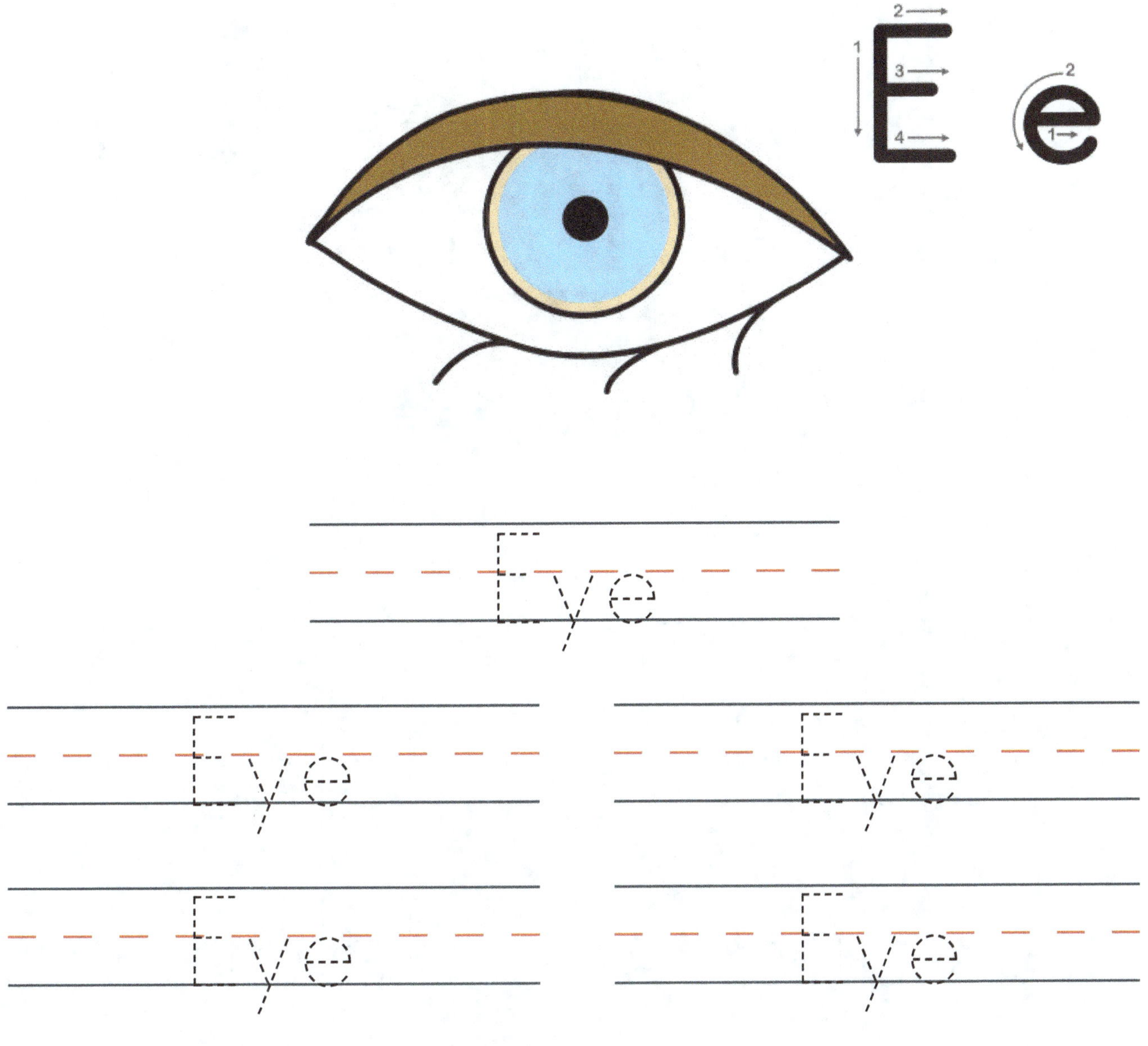

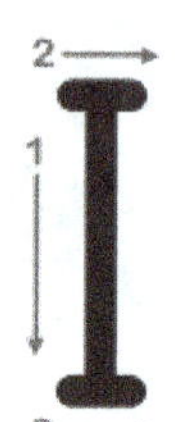

Island

Island

Island

Island

Island

I
i
Ice
Ice
Ice
Ice
Ice

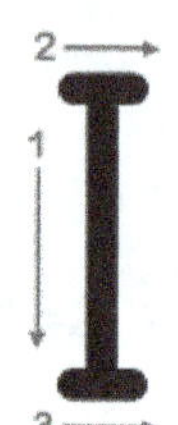

Ice cream

Ice cream

Ice cream

Ice cream

Ice cream

2
1
3
I
i
2
1
Igloo
Igloo
Igloo
Igloo
Igloo

Owl
Owl
Owl
Owl
Owl

Octopus

Octopus

Octopus

Octopus

Octopus

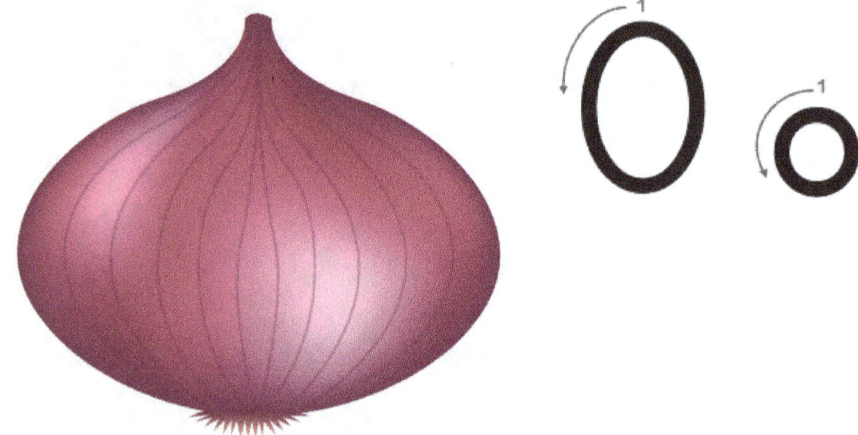

Onion

Onion

Onion

Onion

Onion

O o

Orange

Orange

Orange

Orange

Orange

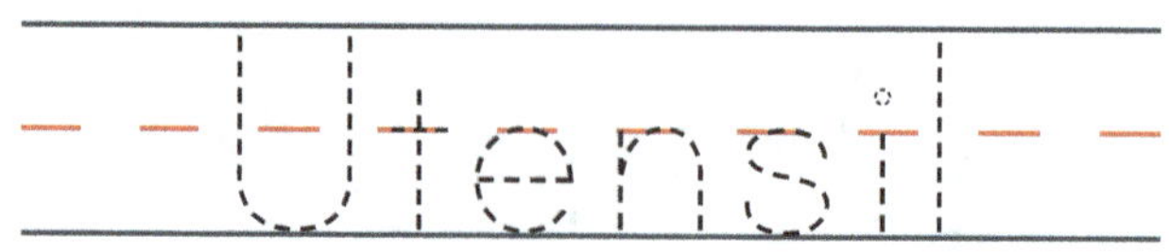
Utensil

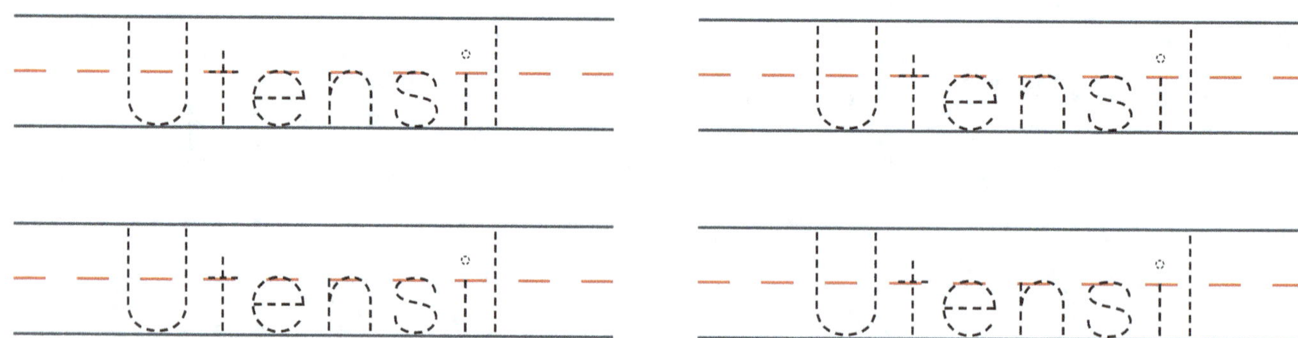
Utensil
Utensil
Utensil
Utensil

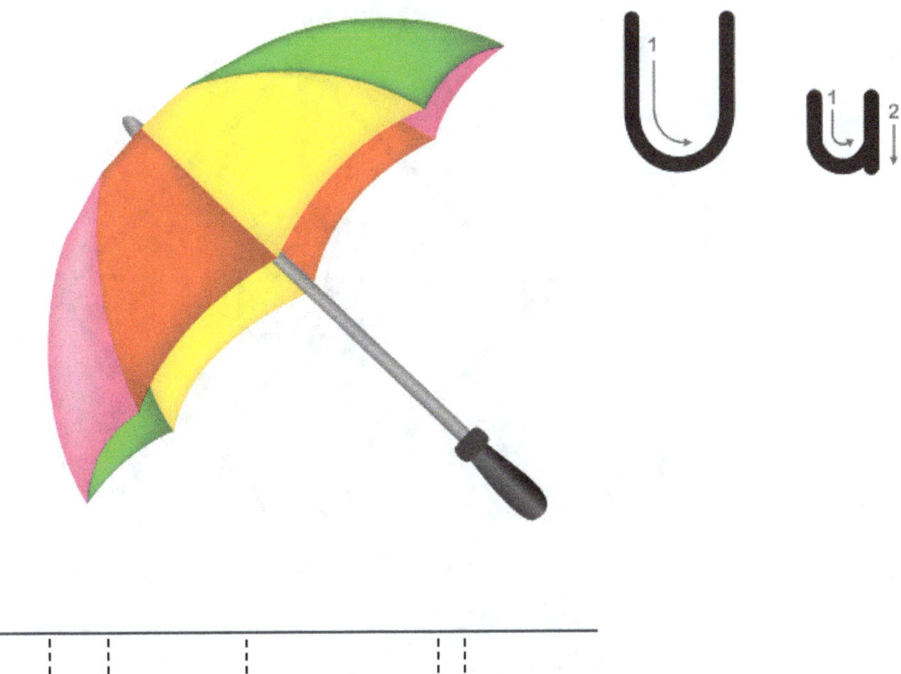

U u

Umbrella

Umbrella Umbrella

Umbrella Umbrella

U
U u
U-turn
U-turn
U-turn
U-turn
U-turn

U u
UFO
UFO
UFO
UFO
UFO

Write the
missing vowel.

CHE___SE

C___R

P___G

B_ELL

FR_EG

SN_EW

WⵣRM

HⵣME

ZⵣBRA

D ___ C K

B ___ R D

S ___ N

F _ S H

R _ N G

L I _ N

HE — RT

SN — KE

SW — N

SQ_IRREL

CL_CK

QU_EN

LA__GH

SCH__OL

BO__T

CR_B

CL_UD

DR__M

FRU__T

TR__IN

KNIF__

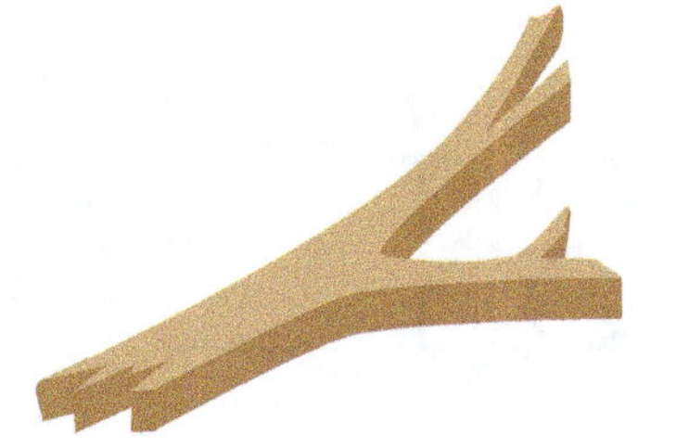

TW__G

STR__ET

SP__NGE

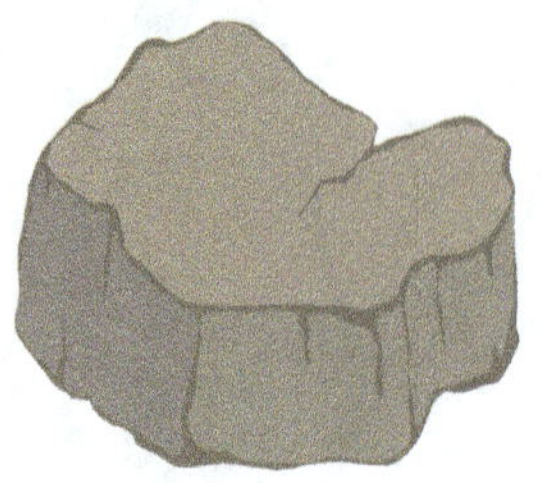

ST_NE

P_NCIL

RA_NBOW

KIT _

GR _ PES

B _ G

Trace and rewrite the words.

astronaut

astronaut

alligator

alligator

apple

apple

Trace and rewrite the words.

elephant elephant

empty empty

eleven eleven

Trace and rewrite the words.

iguana   iguana

insect   insect

igloo   igloo

Trace and rewrite the words.

octopus

octopus

ostrich

ostrich

off

off

Trace and rewrite the words.

under   under

umpire   umpire

umbrella   umbrella

ANSWERS!

CHEESE	RING	DRUM
CAR	LION	FRUIT
PIG	HEART	TRAIN
BALL	SNAKE	KNIFE
FROG	SWAN	TWIG
SNOW	SQUIRREL	STREET
WORM	CLOCK	SPONGE
HOME	QUEEN	STONE
ZEBRA	LAUGH	PENCIL
DUCK	SCHOOL	RAINBOW
BIRD	BOAT	KITE
SUN	CRAB	GRAPES
FISH	CLOUD	BUG

Visit
BABY PROFESSOR
EDUCATION KIDS
www.BabyProfessorBooks.com
to download Free Baby Professor eBooks
and view our catalog of new and exciting
Children's Books